Revelation

EXPLORING GOD'S REDEMPTIVE PLAN

BEACON HILL PRESS

OF KANSAS CITY

Revelation
EXPLORING GOD'S REDEMPTIVE PLAN

Editor
Mike L. Wonch
Director of Curriculum
Merritt J. Nielson
Director of Editorial
Bonnie Perry
Writer
Carol Rotz

All scripture quotations, unless otherwise indicated, are taken from the *Holy Bible, International Version*®, (NIV®). Copyright © 1973, 1978, 1984, 2011 by Biblica, Inc. Used by permission of Zondervan. All rights reserved worldwide.

King James Version (KJV)

Copyright 2014 by Beacon Hill Press of Kansas City

ISBN: 978-0-8341-3143-9
Printed in U.S.A.

10 9 8 7 6 5 4 3 2 1

CONTENTS

Introduction	4
1. Why Study Revelation?	6
2. Principles of Interpretation	14
3. Seven Churches	22
4. Symbolism	30
5. Christ in Revelation	38
6. Hymns of Revelation	46
7. Judgment and Restoration	54
Notes	62

No other book of the Bible has caused as much misunderstanding, confusion, and debate as Revelation. Why? It may be its symbolic language, its visions, or its apocalyptic genre. Throughout the centuries, Bible scholars, theologians, and laymen have studied its words and attempted to understand its message to first-century Christians, its message for Christians today, and its message for the future of humankind.

Unlike some resources, *Revelation: Exploring God's Redemptive Plan* does not presume to outline the events surrounding the end of days. It is not designed to be a map or timeline for the end of the world. However, each chapter will help you understand what this apocalyptic book has to say to us now and in the future. This study will help you understand that Revelation is not so much about doom and gloom as it is about the glory of God and His redemptive plan for humankind.

As you read each page, may the message of Revelation come alive in your heart and life, and may you live every day in light of John's prayer, "Amen. Come, Lord Jesus."

Rev. Carol Rotz, D. Litt. et Phil., served in education as a missionary for the Church of the Nazarene in South Africa, Kenya, and Papua New Guinea. She retired from Northwest Nazarene University, where she taught New Testament and was chair of the Department of Religion. She continues to teach internationally and as an adjunct professor for NNU.

Why Study Revelation?

"Blessed is the one who reads aloud the words of this prophecy, and blessed are those who hear it and take to heart what is written in it, because the time is near."

(Revelation 1:3)

In this first chapter we will acknowledge the difficulty of studying Revelation and begin an exploration of the blessings in store for those who accept the challenge. Revelation is difficult because it is a prophetic, apocalyptic letter that, like wisdom literature,[1] requires careful consideration. In fact, it is so difficult to interpret that many have stopped trying. If you are one of them, you are not alone. John Wesley, an eighteenth-century theologian, pastor, and forefather of the Wesleyan movement, understood that some of Revelation might not be grasped until eternity. Yet he encouraged all to "bless God for the measure of light we may enjoy, and improve it to his glory."[2]

Reflect on this...

Take a moment to reflect on your experience with and understanding of Revelation. What words come to mind when you think of Revelation?

So, why should we study Revelation? The answer is simple: because it is "the Word of God" from Jesus about His gift to us now and for the future. This last book of the Bible is there for a reason, and the book itself declares that those who read and obey its message will be blessed (Revelation 1:3; see 12:17). There were, of course, no printing presses or copy machines in the first century, and many people could not read. The word "read" in 1:3 means specifically to "read aloud," and that's what happened. A courier would travel from church to church and read the message to the assembled congregations.

---

1. We will unpack each of those terms.
2. Wesley, John. "Notes on the Revelation of Jesus Christ." *The Wesley Center Online.* 1993-2011. Northwest Nazarene University. 5 May 2013. www.wesley.nnu.edu.

The dramatic nature of the book comes through in such a reading, and the messenger would answer questions from those gathered to increase their understanding. The blessing is promised to those who read, hear, and obey its message. In order to obey what is contained in Revelation we need to grasp what it says, and that requires study.

Let's acknowledge that the book is difficult. Let's admit that it's easier to be blessed by studying the Lord's Prayer or the fruit of the Spirit. Let's also recognize that this often-quoted book is one of the most misunderstood in the Bible. We need to study it so that we aren't confused by inadequate, unhelpful, or even harmful ideas about Revelation. We need to study it so that we can mine its riches. Revelation is not some strange, futuristic tale of gloom and doom. It has a message for us today—a message of warning, encouragement, challenge, and hope. How sad that so many in the Church miss out on the important truths God has revealed to us through this challenging book! Let's look at some of the reasons people shy away from Revelation.

Probably the main things we find difficult in Revelation are its unusual images and characters. It would be easier if we lived in the first century, since this type of writing was popular for several hundred years around the time of Christ. The English word "revelation" is similar to the Greek *apocalypsis,* which means "uncovering," "disclosure," or "revelation." This word is used in the very first verse of Revelation to describe the book as a message from God to uncover the truth about evil and judgment, Christ and salvation. Revelation is not written in some secret code that only certain people can understand. Its purpose is not to obscure, but to explain.

This ancient form of writing includes visions with symbols that morph and have several levels of meaning. Like other ancient apocalypses,[3] Revelation

---

3. For example, the Syriac Apocalypse of Baruch.

uses symbolic, poetic language that does not spell out meaning, but paints multi-layered word pictures. For example, in Revelation 1:10, John reports hearing a voice, and when he turns around to see who is speaking, he sees seven lampstands and someone "like a son of man" (1:12-13). In 1:20, we learn that the lampstands represent the churches and that the individual must be Jesus. However, the description of Him in verses 12-18 does not sound like a carpenter from Nazareth. The vision in 1:12-18 is packed with details that are derived from the Old Testament, as well as Greek and Roman figures of speech and express the nature of Christ. For example, His eyes are "like blazing fire." Greek and Latin writings used this comparison to speak of the eyes of their gods, and Daniel 10:6 tells of a heavenly being with eyes "like flaming torches." From this there is no doubt that the figure is divine, and the other details combine in a powerful representation of the risen Christ.

Revelation is difficult because, like this first vision, the book conveys truth in unusual ways. Like other apocalypses, it includes heavenly messengers, symbolic numbers, and epic battles. Revelation also includes visions of violence and upheaval, and we need to consider them. But Revelation is not the story of a grim war between good and evil where evil seems unbeatable. God is not struggling against an equal; the future is not in question. God the Father has triumphed over evil through Jesus Christ. Forty-six times John sees God sitting triumphantly on a throne in heaven surrounded by creatures, elders, and angels. All creation joins in their praise to God the Father and Jesus the Lamb (5:11-14).

Though God's mighty presence and actions in the past confirm divine direction in the present and guarantee the future. God's purposes for humanity depend on our response. Unlike most apocalyptic literature, Revelation is not anonymous. It is personal. John is a spirit-led (1:10) servant of God (1:1), a brother and fellow-sufferer with those for whom the book was originally written (1:9). We can relate to his astonishment at the visions he sees and his struggle to put the indescribable into words. For example, he often hears loud voices from heaven that sound like "a trumpet" (1:9), "rushing waters" (1:15), and "thunder" (6:1).

Revelation's apocalyptic form presents a multitude of challenges, but it is helpful to remember that it is also a letter. Chapters 2 and 3 of Revelation contain letters to seven churches that represent the entire Church, and the book as a whole is also a letter. Read Revelation 1:4-5 and compare it with Galatians 1:1-5. If you are familiar with the other New Testament letters, you will recognize this style of opening ancient letters.

When is the last time you wrote or received a handwritten letter? I enjoy receiving them and try to write at least one note of appreciation or encouragement each week. But texting and various social media have almost made the old-fashioned letter a quaint, nostalgic museum piece that has very little impact on our lives. For many, Revelation has been set aside in a similar way. But you say, "Revelation is just strange—I've never received a letter like that." And you are right. The letter is filled with extraordinary characters and events that describe the end of history in a variety of bizarre ways—its apocalyptic form is difficult. Additionally, since it is a letter to the first-century churches, we need to keep in mind the circumstances of those churches. In the first century, the Roman Empire both opposed Christian living and promoted a culture that tempted Christians to compromise their faith. Like today, some endured severe persecution.

Reflect on this...

What temptations and dangers do Christians face today?

Revelation challenges us to see a different reality—one in which the powerful opponents of the Church are already defeated. In this authentic view of reality, true power is demonstrated by Jesus' sacrifice on the cross. In this world where evil seems so dominant, Revelation calls us to follow Jesus in lives of self-sacrifice and witness in contrast to lifestyles that emphasize power, riches, and self-gratification. We who are the spiritual descendants of the first recipients of Revelation need its message of caution, encouragement, and hope.

Another challenge in studying Revelation is that in addition to being a letter written in apocalyptic style, it is also prophecy (1:3). Like Revelation as a whole, biblical prophecy is often misunderstood. It is not like using a crystal ball or other means to see the future. Rather than describing a predetermined sequence of events, it calls us to live responsibly in the present by revealing the consequences of our choices. Read, for example, Revelation 21:6-8. Instead of foretelling the future, the prophet proclaims God's Word. Revelation does not give a timeline for what is to come, but it does show the culmination of God's plan for humanity to live fully in His presence. Then God will wipe away our tears, and there will be no death, mourning, crying or pain (7:17; 21:4). God's glory will provide light to all the nations through Christ, who is the lamp (21:23-24). These final visions offer only glimpses or perspectives of that magnificent reality, but their beauty draws us to live with hope and expectation of that promise.

> We who are the spiritual descendants of the first recipients of Revelation need its message of caution, encouragement, and hope.

In fact, the future has already broken into the present. In Revelation, voices in heaven proclaim, "The kingdom of the world has become the kingdom of our Lord and of his Messiah, and he will reign for ever and ever" (11:15; see also 12:10). God's kingdom has begun, but it is not all it will be in the future. Revelation 21 describes that future fellowship as a marriage supper (19:9), and the Church as a bride who is united with her husband, Christ (21:9). In another metaphor, the New Jerusalem comes down to earth from heaven, and all are invited to enter the city of peace. Through these images, the reader is invited to join in eager anticipation for the return of Christ. In the very last verse of Revelation, Christ gives assurance of His return, and our response can only echo the final words of the book: "Come, Lord Jesus" (22:20). ●

NOTES

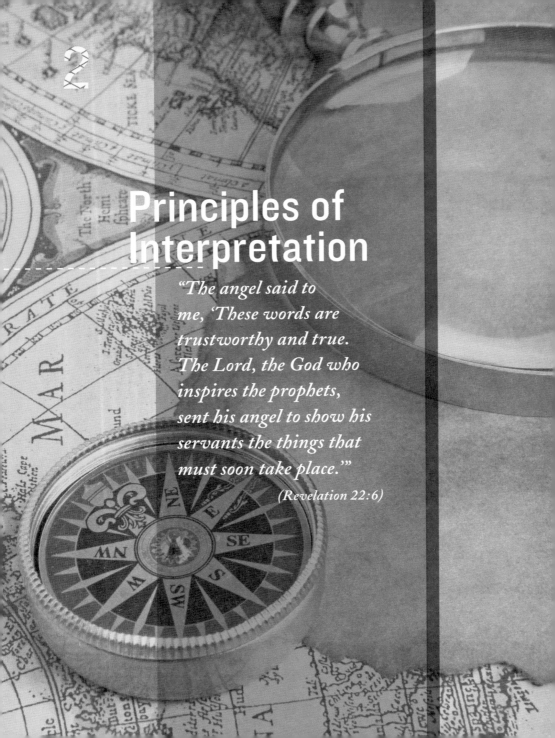

Principles of Interpretation

"The angel said to me, 'These words are trustworthy and true. The Lord, the God who inspires the prophets, sent his angel to show his servants the things that must soon take place.'"

(Revelation 22:6)

As we study Revelation, we need to keep in mind that it is just that—a revelation of God's purposes for humanity. Its form is difficult for us, but its message is so important we need to do the study necessary to hear and respond to God's call. How do we deal with the disturbing images, confusing plot line, and fluid symbolism? First, we need to realize that the visions are more like works of art than news reports. Revelation presents a different understanding of the world, one in which God calls us to live our lives in anticipation of the future prepared for those who accept the adventure of following Jesus. It challenges us to believe that God's kingdom has already begun, even when evil seems to be winning.

This, however, does not explain all of the images, characters, and episodes that cannot be pinned down as concretely as we would like. There are so many conflicting teachings about Revelation that it is difficult to know who to believe or how to interpret it. In this chapter, we will first look at the main ways Revelation has been interpreted in the past, then consider some guidelines for studying it for ourselves.

> **Revelation presents a different understanding of the world, one in which God calls us to live our lives in anticipation of the future prepared for those who accept the adventure of following Jesus.**

Historically, there have been four main ways of studying Revelation. The first, known as the **preterist**, was first developed in 1614 and relates the entire book to its first-century setting. Based on the fall of Babylon in Revelation 14-18, interpreters in this category believe that the book tells the fate of either Israel or the Roman Empire. If Israel is the focus, the lesson is that Israel would be punished because it broke God's covenant. If the Roman Empire is the focus, the letter would serve to assure early Christians that their persecutor would be judged. The difficulty of this view is that it limits the message to the early church. In that case, we would study the book only for its insights into that time and place.

The second approach is the **historicist** view. There are many versions of this view, depending on who or what is identified as the greatest evil during the historical period of the interpreter. In this scheme, Revelation's symbols are matched with historical people and events that end with the historicist's own day. Since its beginning in the 13th century, the pope, Mohammed, Hitler, and many others have been identified as the evil one. The problem is that the assignment of symbols is arbitrary and limited to the time frame of each interpreter, most of whom disagree. Also, the perspective is generally limited by Western events that would have had no bearing upon the first-century Christians.

The third approach, the **futurist view**, misunderstands prophecy as a prediction of the future. In this perspective, everything after the third chapter of Revelation refers to a future time immediately before Christ's return. There are several futurist systems with slightly different timetables, but the following scheme is typical: the period begins with the restoration of the nation of Israel, then a secret rapture. A seven-year tribulation and the Antichrist's reign follow. Then the evil nations gather to fight over Jerusalem, and Christ returns to reign for one thousand years. Finally, Christ defeats Satan and his followers, and there is a new heaven and earth where Christ and His followers rule.

Like the historicists, the futurists attempt to demonstrate that the end is near by looking for people and events to correlate with the book's symbols. In addition, they take verses out of context, compile them into a particular system, and interpret them literally. For example, the seven years of tribulation is taken from Daniel's week of years (Daniel 9:27), and neither "rapture" nor "Antichrist" appear in Revelation. Unfortunately, since its beginning in the 19th century, the futurist view has been quite popular. If we understand Revelation this way, it has meaning only if we are living through the last years as outlined by this perspective. It would have had no meaning for the early church for whom it was originally written or anyone up to the present day.

The fourth approach, called **idealist**, highlights Revelation's symbolism. It stresses the theological core of Revelation and holds that it is a timeless drama of the battle between good and evil. An extreme version of this view holds that Revelation merely depicts this struggle with no reference to historical events. But Revelation is firmly rooted in the life, death, and resurrection of Jesus. An extreme idealist view would not include Christ's return or judgment and rewards.

Reflect on this...

If you had to choose one of these approaches to interpreting Revelation, which would it be—preterist, historicist, futurist, or idealist?

Fortunately, we do not have to elect a winner and use it exclusively. Though all the approaches to studying Revelation are inadequate, each has something to contribute to a well-balanced understanding of this complicated book. The rest of this chapter will present guidelines for studying Revelation that incorporate insights from the four historical views.

1. **Remember that Revelation was written to first-century Christians.** They were real people with hopes and fears, struggling to live a life centered in God, but in many ways their world was different from ours.

2. **Remember that Revelation can speak to us today.** The message was not just for those early Christians. God's Word truly is alive and active (Hebrews 4:12) and continues to speak to us. It shows spiritual realities and the future God has planned for us. We need to listen to Revelation's challenges and promises, to allow it to evaluate us and our situation in light of eternity; we will be blessed if we obey it (Revelation 1:3).

3. **Remember that God is at work fulfilling His divine plan for humanity.** The kingdom of heaven has already begun; it begins when we invite God to lead us day by day. In a real sense, the "last days" began with the death and resurrection of Christ, and anticipation of His return continues to draw us forward to the full realization of God's kingdom.

4. **Remember that the visions, not their content, are sequential.** In Revelation, John often reports what takes place next. We must understand that he is reporting the sequence of his experiences rather than a historical timeline.

5. **Remember that the symbols in Revelation represent important truths.** John's visions are visual messages, not historical accounts. Dragons and beasts, a lion and a lamb represent more horrible and more wonderful realities that are better shown than told. Be careful, though. Don't try to assign a meaning to every detail.

6. **Remember the rest of the Bible.** In form, Revelation is very different from other New Testament books, but its message is not. Revelation's teachings fit with what the rest of the Bible teaches about God and salvation, and

it refers to the Old Testament over 500 times to help us understand its message.

7. **Remember that one of the best ways to understand the Bible is to interact with it by posing questions about its content.** Sometimes we are able to find the answers to those questions ourselves, but often we need assistance. Good study Bibles, commentaries, and word studies can help. Be careful to make sure, though, that the sources used are not stuck in one of the four inadequate schools of thought mentioned above.

This week read Revelation 1:12-16 and take time to reflect on these questions in relation to John's vision.

- *How might the first-century Christians have understood this passage? How does it relate to the situation in the first-century? How is our situation similar or different?*
  - ○ The details of John's description were familiar in first-century Mediterranean culture. Lampstands, robes with sashes, the use of bronze and swords, and their symbolism would have made sense to the early Christians.
- *What truths do these images represent? Are the details important?*
  - ○ The details contribute to an understanding of the majesty, power, purity, wisdom, and love of the risen Christ. But their individual meaning is not as important as the whole picture.
- *How does the meaning of this passage relate to the rest of Revelation? The rest of the New Testament? The rest of the Bible? Is it saying the same thing or giving a different perspective?*
  - ○ The individual symbols appear in other parts of Revelation. They remind us of this entire first vision and draw us to the centrality of Christ throughout the book.

- There is no description of Jesus' physical appearance elsewhere in the New Testament, and there is none here—it is symbolic.
- *How is this truth taught elsewhere in the Bible? Are there references to the Old Testament? If so, what do those references indicate?*
  - In this first vision in Revelation there are many Old Testament references.
- *What is God's message to us through this passage? What is God saying to us as the Church? What is our responsibility?*
  - In response to this magnificent vision of Jesus, John "fell at his feet as though dead" (1:17). If we truly understand who Jesus is, we will also be awed and humbled in His presence.

These questions help us to begin to truly listen to the text and unwrap its meaning. Keep in mind the principles outlined above as we explore the fascinating visions filled with symbols and insights for us as the Church. ●

Reflect on this...

How will this chapter help you as you read Revelation in the future?

NOTES:

3

Seven Churches

"Write on a scroll what you see and send it to the seven churches: to Ephesus, Smyrna, Pergamum, Thyatira, Sardis, Philadelphia and Laodicea."

(Revelation 1:11)

In Chapter 1 of our study, we established that Revelation is an ancient letter sent to seven churches in what is now Turkey (see 1:4). Its message from God, conveyed through visions, continues to be relevant for us as the Church.

The seven churches represent the many other first-century churches. We don't know why they were chosen, although they may have been a mail route. The messenger would have read the entire book, including all the letters, to each church he visited. Like our churches today, each was rooted in a particular mix of social, economic, religious, and political factors. The Roman Empire demanded allegiance, and being a good citizen sometimes conflicted with Christian values. The Empire also provided economic opportunities, but the mandatory trade guilds included pagan feasts to their patron Greek or Roman deity. Every city boasted temples to a variety of such gods whose worship included immoral practices. Each church had its own challenges in relationship to these and other cultural elements. The city of Ephesus, for example, had a complex setting, including a long history of hostility between Jews and Gentiles. Ephesus was notorious for its association with magic, emperor worship, and worship of the Greek goddess Artemis.

John's first vision (1:12-16) introduces the risen Christ, who is identified as the author of the letters we will be considering in this chapter. Elements of this description appear in other parts of Revelation including the letters to the churches in Chapters 2 and 3. After the command to write, each letter includes a description of Jesus.[4]

---

4. The descriptions in the letters to Smyrna and Laodicea do not come from the vision but from 1:8 and 1:5.

Reflect on this...

Reread Revelation 1:12–16 and then the following verses:

- *Ephesus: 2:1*
- *Pergamum: 2:12*
- *Thyatira: 2:18*
- *Sardis: 3:1*
- *Philadelphia: 3:7*

Compare the designations for Christ with the vision. How do they portray Jesus? How does knowing Jesus in this way affect the church today?

The letters have other things in common besides the command to write and the description of Christ. All the churches except Laodicea are given a commendation for the works they are doing. It is faith in action that is praised. For example, the Christians at Thyatira are commended for their increasing love, faith, service, and perseverance. The church in Pergamum is commended for faithfulness to Christ in the face of severe persecution. The Philadelphians model patient endurance. The confirmation of the Smyrnans' wealth implies perseverance in spite of their suffering.

Another theme in the letters is criticism for such things as tolerating false teaching (Pergamum and Thyatira) and lack of zeal (Sardis and Laodicea). Only Smyrna and Philadelphia do not receive a rebuke, although they both faced false Jews and the devil brought suffering to Smyrna. Other foes had more success. The Nicolaitans in Pergamum, false apostles in Ephesus, and

Jezebel in Thyatira threatened to lead Christians away from true worship of God. Failure in other churches came from wrong emphases. In their zeal for good theology, the Ephesians forgot that the primary characteristic of the Christian is love. The church in Pergamum failed where the Ephesians excelled. Their faulty thinking led to actions that did not match their profession of faith. Bad theology was not the problem at Sardis. They knew the gospel and its requirements, but they were not living up to God's standard.

Reflect on this...

How do you think Christ would commend the Church in general and your church in particular? Would the commendations be the same or different from those given to the early churches?

According to Revelation, the remedy for the churches' problems was (and is) repentance. If they did not repent, they would suffer the consequences. Christ would remove the Ephesians' lampstand. A church that loses its focus eventually dies and ceases to be a church. Jesus threatened to come to Laodicea like a thief and spit the lukewarm out of His mouth. Neither hot like the medicinal springs nor cold like a refreshing drink, they were good for nothing. In Pergamum, He would make war on the followers of Balaam and the Nicolaitans with the sword of His mouth. False teachings must be combated with the truth of the gospel. In Thyatira, He would kill Jezebel and her followers with tribulation and pestilence. The axiom, "You've made your bed, now lie in it" comes to mind. Sinful choices have consequences.

Reflect on this...

How do you feel about the call to repentance? How does it work in the Church today?

Christ provided instructions to strengthen the spiritual life of the individual churches depending on their needs. The most specific is the injunction to the Laodiceans to buy symbolic gold, white garments and eye salve from Christ. They thought they were rich, but in the midst of the wealth of Laodicea, they were spiritually poor. In a city known for a famous medical school and healing eye salve, they were spiritually blind. Despite the flourishing local textile industry, they were spiritually naked. The other churches were advised to remember from where they had fallen and what they had received. They were challenged to wake up, to be faithful, to hold fast, and to passionately live out their faith.

These judgments, warnings, and instructions challenge us to be ready for whatever may come, some of which is detailed later in the book. They also show God's faithfulness. God judges the finally impenitent, but constantly and consistently urges repentance while there is still time. The tribulation and testing are instruments of mercy and salvation for those who will respond. Like the church of the first century, we are called to persevere. Like Ephesus (2:2-3), we must endure hardships and combat false teachers. Like Thyatira (2:19), we are to do works of service. Like Philadelphia (3:8), some of us must persist through persecution. We are all called to be vessels God can use to save others (11:1-14) and ultimately to rule with God (2:26ff; 3:21; 20:4-6). We all must follow Jesus as faithful witnesses (1:5; 3:14; 14:4). And we are assured that along with these great responsibilities come the rewards for those who remain faithful (2:7; 11, 17, 26; 3:5, 12, 21; 20:6; 21:27).

All the letters conclude with a call to "those who have ears to hear what the Spirit says to the churches." It is a plea to listen carefully to what has been said. The invitation is for us as well.

Reflect on this...

How does the Spirit speak to churches today? Share an example.

Those who do respond to the Spirit's voice and are victorious receive heavenly rewards. They will not be hurt by the second death (2:11). Physical death comes to all, but spiritual death is a choice. They will "eat of the tree of life" (2:7) and will be given "some of the hidden manna" (2:17). These symbols of nourishment show the abundant provision in Christ. Jesus will give them "a white stone with a new name" (2:17) and will write on them the name of His God, the city of His God, and His new name (3:12). These emblems of identification assure eternal fellowship with God. They will be "dressed in white" (3:5) to show their purity. Christ will acknowledge the names that are in "the book of life" before His Father and the angels (3:5). Citizenship in God's kingdom reflects a personal relationship. God will give them "authority over the nations" (2:26) and "the morning star" (2:28). This authorization is to carry out the purposes of Christ who is himself "the Morning Star" (22:16). He will make them "pillars in the temple" (3:12). In other words, the victorious will have intimate fellowship with God, who is the heavenly temple

(21:22). In another metaphor of intimacy, they are granted "the right to sit" with Christ on His throne—the very throne of God (3:21).

> When we accept the perspective of Christ in the letters, repentance, perseverance, and faithfulness become acts of love to God, and victory is assured.

In the light of these incentives, how could anyone not set their course with single-minded determination to overcome all obstacles and be victorious? The rewards are so ample, the requirements so clear. How could anyone miss the way? As the visions unfold, the reasons become all too obvious. The opponents are deceptive. Their allure is very real. Though the pressures and difficulties are all but overwhelming, God provides His followers with a seal that assures His provision and protection. However, it does not exempt them from tribulation. Martyrs cry out for an end to their suffering, but in His mercy, God provides opportunity for repentance. It is easy to be distracted by the immediate, by what seems to constitute reality, and ignore the ultimate and eternal reality.

We are invited into this drama. We who are not first-time readers know the outcome, but we are constantly drawn into the conflict. We read of cosmic battles in a first-century context, but we are continually surprised by disturbing contemporary applications and implications. It is the humanity of the seven churches that helps us to identify with both their plight and their faith in God. When we accept the perspective of Christ in the letters, repentance, perseverance, and faithfulness become acts of love to God, and victory is assured. ●

NOTES:

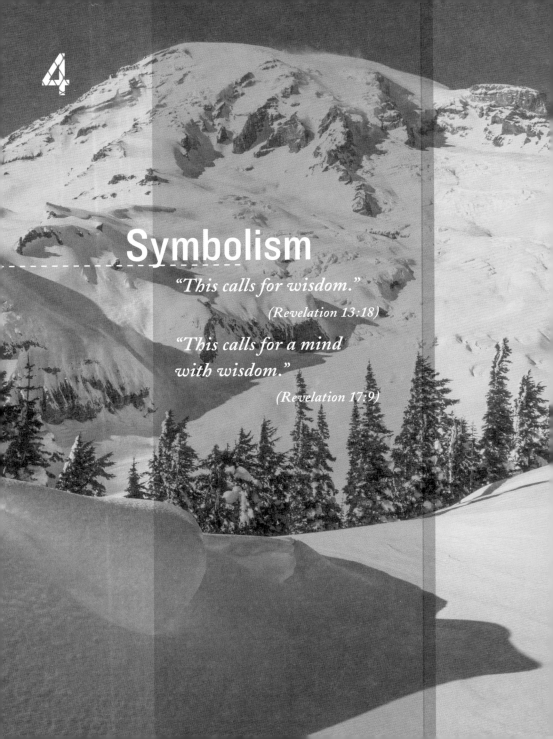

4

Symbolism

"This calls for wisdom."

(Revelation 13:18)

"This calls for a mind with wisdom."

(Revelation 17:9)

In the first chapter of Revelation, John explains that seven lampstands represent seven churches (1:20). It makes sense in this first vision, where a wise and powerful Savior moves among His people. The image and clarification prepare us for the letters to the churches from this same Lord. In a later vision, John explains that the seven heads of the beast are "the seven hills on which the woman sits" (17:9). This image is not as straightforward. One symbol is replaced by another, and as the verse says, "This calls for a mind with wisdom."[5] First-century people of the Roman Empire would have recognized the seven hills as a reference to Rome because of its geographic location literally on seven hills. This Greek word for "hills" elsewhere refers to mountains that symbolize strength. In the Old Testament, mountains signify kingdoms or kings. This Old Testament link to kings is highlighted by a second explanation in verse 10 that the "heads are also seven kings." This and the rest of verse 10 also call for wisdom.[6]

Although the symbolic language of Revelation is complicated by our cultural and historical distance, the figures of speech themselves are familiar to us. In this chapter, we will consider how figurative language works and look at several types of symbolism used in Revelation.

> Although the symbolic language of Revelation is complicated by our cultural and historical distance, the figures of speech themselves are familiar to us.

5. Remember our discussion in chapter 1 of this study that Revelation is like the wisdom literature of the Old Testament (for example, Ecclesiastes). It does not state things in a straightforward manner like the Ten Commandments. Its word pictures and poetic language require thoughtful consideration of the figures of speech, the culture, and the historical context.
6. The statement that "five have fallen" implies that they have been overthrown or died violently, and fits with the deaths of many of the Roman emperors. The attempts that have been made to match these five with first-century Roman emperors are not satisfactory because it is difficult to know who to begin with and who should be included.

Figurative language uses words in ways that differ to some extent from their ordinary meaning in everyday usage. They express meaning in a vivid and striking manner that makes them more effective. Just as salt brings out the flavor of food, they add interest and zest. They add a liveliness that attracts attention. Proverbs, for example, are a part of every culture. Traditional English ones include "When in Rome, do as the Romans do" and "A picture is worth a thousand words."

Reflect on this...

What other sayings come to mind? What would a person need to know to understand them?

What significance might the two sayings listed above have for our study of Revelation?

The symbolic language of Revelation works in similar ways. We need to understand not only the meaning of the words themselves, but also what they suggest. The first example above does not mean we are to pattern our lives according to the practices of the Romans, ancient or modern. Rather, it advises a visitor anywhere to respect and adapt to local customs. In our study, knowing ancient Roman customs will help us understand Revelation. The second example is especially appropriate for our study; visions consisting of thought-provoking pictures require many words to analyze.

Common figures of speech in Revelation include the simile, metaphor, metonymy (meh-TA-nuh-mee), and synecdoche (se-NEK-du-kee). Even if we do not know these terms, we are familiar with how they work because they are used in everyday speech and writing.

First, a *simile* associates one person, place, thing, or idea to another so that the main word is made clearer. It is easy to spot a simile because the two ideas are linked with "like" or "as." John often uses similes to describe his visions. For example, the voice of one of the four living creatures that surround the throne in heaven sounded to John "like thunder" (6:1); the singing of the 144,000 seemed "like a loud peal of thunder" (14:2); and the shouting of a great multitude was "like loud peals of thunder" (19:6).[7] These voices could be described as loud, deafening, roaring, booming, crashing, or rolling; but likening them to thunder says it all.

Sometimes John omits the connecting "like" or "as" and makes the comparison more directly as a *metaphor*. A metaphor simply substitutes one person, place, thing, or idea for another so that their resemblance is implied. John's description of the throne in heaven includes "flashes of lightning, rumblings and peals of thunder" (4:5) coming from the throne. Like Old Testament poetry, this thunderstorm symbolizes the power and glory of the Lord. Jewish Christians would also remember these as signs of God's presence on Mt. Sinai (Exodus 19:16-25). People in Asia Minor would recognize the thunderbolt as a symbol of the Greek god Zeus and the Roman god Jupiter. It also suggested the deification of Roman emperors, who were sometimes depicted holding a thunderbolt as a scepter. These thunderstorm metaphors occur in several other visions in Revelation (see 8:5; 11:19; 16:18), each time to emphasize God's power.

---

7. This last sound from heaven actually was described by three similes: "like a great multitude, like the roar of rushing waters and like loud peals of thunder" (Rev 19:6).

Reflect on this...

Among the many metaphors of Revelation is that the Church is a bride. Read Revelation 19:7 and 21:2. What do these metaphors tell us about the Church?

Another figure of speech often used in Revelation is *metonymy*—a literary device in which two ideas are so related that the mention of one suggests the other. For example, in 1:12, John heard a voice and "turned around to see" it. Of course, a voice cannot be seen, and it is not the voice itself that John is looking for; rather, because the voice is closely associated with the one to whom it belongs, the use of the word "voice" implies "the person speaking."

Synecdoche works a bit differently: in this figure of speech, a constituent part of something stands for the whole, or the whole is used to refer to a part. For example, three times in Revelation the Lord declares, "I am the Alpha and Omega" (1:8; 21:6; 22:13). These first and last letters of the Greek alphabet imply the inclusion of everything in between. They indicate that God is the beginning and end of all things.

A fascinating and much-used form of synecdoche is the symbolic use of numbers. Reflecting their usage in many ancient cultures, numbers in Revelation represent general lengths of time or ideas that are based on commonly accepted meanings. One well-known example is the number seven. This is the number of days in which God created the universe, culminating in the Sabbath rest (Genesis 2:1-3). Therefore, "seven" represents natural and divine completeness or perfection. In a similar way, "ten," the number of our fingers and toes, expresses human completion. Twelve, the number of tribes in the Old Testament and disciples in the New Testament, symbolizes all of God's people. Multiplication of the numbers intensifies their meaning. The 144,000 who receive God's seal of identification and protection represent the entirety of those who follow Jesus rather than a literal number. The symbolism is heightened by multiplying 12 times 12, and then multiplying 144 by 1,000, an intensification of ten.

Reflect on this...

Read Revelation 7:1. Consider the three uses of the number " four." What do you think the number represents?

- ○ *It was common in ancient thought to divide the earth into fourths, so the four corners would symbolize universality. Winds in the Old Testament represent judgment (see, for example, Jeremiah 23:19).*

Another well-known symbolic number is 666, "the number of the beast" that is also "the number of a man" (13:18). "A man" may refer to an individual who the early Christians would have known. More probably the phrase "the number of a man" means human calculation. The number six represents human effort and, in contrast to the perfect seven, incompleteness. Humanity falls short of God's perfection, so the use of the number three times symbolizes human striving without God. The results are failure, more failure, and still more failure. This mark of the beast contrasts with God's protective seal on the 144,000 and identifies its bearers as followers of Satan.

It is easy to get caught up in the images of Revelation, but it is a mistake to extract them from their context within the visions and strive to see their literal fulfillment in the first century, or worse yet, the present or future. For example, the number 666[8] has been used to identify many historical figures as the "Antichrist" (remember, that term does not occur in Revelation).

Reflect on this...

Who have you seen identified as the Antichrist, and why do you think that identification was made?

- *1 John identifies "the antichrist" as "whoever denies that Jesus is the Christ" (2:22) and that many antichrists have already come (2:18). In light of this context, many historical figures fit this description. Unfortunately, it is easy to find institutions and individuals who deny that Jesus is Lord.*

Poetic language calls for wisdom. It combines a range of interconnected meanings to form richly textured patterns of significance. We must understand the first-century context through the lens of biblical and historical allusions and compare them with our contemporary situations and relationships. John's visions remind us that a picture truly is worth a thousand words. ●

---

8. In Hebrew, Greek, and Latin, the letters of the alphabet also functioned as numbers. *Gematria*, a system of coded wordplay, was a popular use of these corollaries. In this system, words and names were represented by the sum of their numerical equivalents, but working backward from only a total number yields a range of possibilities.

NOTES:

5

Christ in Revelation

"Worthy is the Lamb, who was slain, to receive power and wealth and wisdom and strength and honor and glory and praise!"

(Revelation 5:12)

Most people would not go to this last book of the New Testament to understand who Jesus is. Yet Revelation has a wealth of meaningful, glorious information about Him that complements what is found in the rest of the New Testament. The Gospels beautifully portray Jesus' life and teachings and call us to align our lives with His. Acts and the Epistles explain the significance of Christ's life, death, and resurrection, and guide Christians then and now to live Christlike lives. Revelation shows us the Messiah, firmly rooted in the Old Testament, honored with titles, portrayed through visions, acclaimed in worship, and victorious through sacrifice and faithful witness.

Reflect on this...

How would you describe Jesus Christ?

The very first words of Revelation show the centrality of Christ in all that follows. The Greek says that the revelation is "of" Jesus Christ in 1:1. In Greek grammar, the construction can have several meanings. Think of what you mean when, for example, you say, "this book of mine." If you are handing it to someone, it could mean that it is from you, that you are holding the book, or that you own the book. It could also mean that it is a book about you or that you wrote the book. Some translations interpret the phrase in 1:1, "from Jesus Christ." This would indicate that God gave the revelation to Jesus, to an angel, to John who wrote it down for the churches. This makes sense, but look at verse 2. Not only are the visions God's Word, they are "the testimony of Jesus" (1:2). Here again the construction includes several aspects. The visions give testimony about Jesus; they are conveyed through Jesus; and Jesus *is* the faithful witness, giving testimony in all He is and does.

> Revelation shows us the Messiah, firmly rooted in the Old Testament, honored with titles, portrayed through visions, acclaimed in worship, and victorious through sacrifice and faithful witness.

Revelation's poetic language packs a lot of meaning in few words. The titles for Jesus, for example, help us understand His nature. He is "Alpha and Omega, the beginning and the end" (1:8; 21:6; 22:13), "the first and the last" (1:17; 2:8; 22:13). These titles appropriately come at the beginning and end of Revelation. As we discussed in our last study, this figure of speech called synecdoche emphasizes Jesus' sovereignty over history. All things have their origin in Christ; everything is sustained by Him; and all will come to their fulfillment in Him.

These titles are also ascribed to God so that we see the unity of Father and Son. This relationship is further illustrated by Jesus' titles, "Son of God" (2:18) and "word of God" (1:2, 9; 6:9; 20:4). He was God incarnate on earth, and continues to be "the Living One" (1:18) who makes himself known through John's visions as the "faithful witness" (1:5; 3:14). Recalling a favorite metaphor from the Old Testament and the Gospels, He is also the Shepherd of God's people (7:17). In addition, Jesus is "Faithful and True" (19:11), the "King of kings and Lord of lords" (19:16) who reigns with God forever. He is the "Amen" (3:14), the one who brings all things to fruition.

Reflect on this...

Choose one of the above titles and share how it helps you to realize who Jesus is and what that understanding means for your life.

In addition to the above titles, Jesus is the "Messiah" (1:1, 2, 5; 11:15; 12:10; 20:4, 6), a Hebrew word that means "the anointed one" and is translated into Greek as *Christos*. This title for Jesus eventually became a compound name, Jesus Christ. The Jews of Jesus' day expected a warrior Messiah who would conquer, rule as king, and judge the nations. This warrior Messiah is more described in more detail in Revelation 19.

Reflect on this...

Review the image by reading Revelation 19:11-16, where the risen Christ is seen riding a white horse, judging, and waging war. What is your response to this vision?

The picture is not what the Jews expected; Christ is not the typical superhero. His name, "Faithful and True," highlights the justice with which He will judge. This justice is based on His own death, as His bloodstained robe suggests. His name, "Faithful Witness," continues to inspire His army of followers. This contrasts sharply with the horseman in Revelation 6, who also rode a white horse and was "a conqueror bent on conquest." Christ and His followers conquer evil with the power of the gospel of salvation. This "King of kings and Lord of lords" (19:15) will conquer with the sword coming out of His mouth (19:16), that is, His Word. The One who is the Word of God will conquer through His Word.

These transformed images of a warrior Messiah play an important role in John's visions, but the overwhelming Messianic image of Jesus is that of a suffering servant (see Isaiah 53). This paradox is vividly illustrated by John's vision in chapter 5. There he sees God on His throne holding a sealed scroll, and John weeps because no one can open it. Then one of the 24 elders gives him hope that the "Lion of the tribe of Judah, the Root of David" could do it. These Messianic titles from the Old Testament (see Genesis 49:9 and Isaiah 11:1, 10) emphasize Jesus' royal descent, as well as His fulfillment of the warrior Messiah's role. It is His triumph that qualifies Him alone to open the scroll. But what John sees is not a warrior, but a lamb.

Reflect on this...

What comes to mind when you think of Jesus as the Lamb of God?

Whatever John expected, it was probably different from what he saw. Instead of a victorious warrior, he sees a lamb. In fact, "lamb" is the most often-used metaphor for Jesus in Revelation—it occurs 28 times. This in itself is not unusual because rams were often used in the ancient Near East to depict gods. However, this Lamb was not a powerful, triumphant ram. It was an *arnion,* literally, "a little lamb" that looked like it had been slain. Unlike the lambs slaughtered in the temple, He was alive, standing in the center of heaven. What a powerful picture of Jesus as the sacrificial Lamb who was slain and rose again! Through His sacrifice the warrior Messiah gained victory for all who believe in Him, people "from every tribe and language and people and nation" (5:9; see 7:14; 12:11). The blood of battle is His own. This is why He alone is worthy to open the scroll.

The Lamb John saw continues to challenge our image of Jesus—this Lamb had seven horns and seven eyes. Horns were symbols of power in the Old Testament (see, for example, Jer. 48:25), so the seven[9] horns represent the perfection of power. His seven eyes[10] indicate His perception and knowledge that extends throughout the world. We sometimes use words like "omnipotent" and "omniscient" to describe God, but those words do not carry the force of John's symbolic vision. Throughout John's visions, the Lamb acts on behalf of His people, opening seals, being their shepherd, leading them in battle, judging, receiving praise, uniting with His Bride and providing light in the New Jerusalem.

Though the image of Jesus as the Lamb is widespread in Revelation, it is not the only important metaphor. In the chapter on interpretation we considered John's first vision. Much of the imagery in 1:12-16 mirrors Daniel's vision of a heavenly being, including the title "son of man" (see Daniel 7). It is tempting to equate this title to Jesus' humanity since He is also called "Son of God." The two would highlight Jesus' divine-human being. However, because of the accompanying images of power in Daniel and Revelation, "son of man" more likely reflects Jesus as a heavenly being.[11] In Revelation 14:14, the "son of man" is pictured seated on a cloud-throne, wearing a gold crown, ready to judge the world.

Jesus, the highest and most complete revelation of the character of God, is the central figure in the book of Revelation, adored in heaven and on earth. In the final chapter He verifies that He is "the Alpha and the Omega, the First and the Last, the Beginning and the End" (22:13); "the Root and the

---

9. See the discussion of numbers in the chapter on symbolism.
10. See the discussion of Rev 1:12-16 in the chapter on interpretation.
11. "Son of Man" was an exalted figure in contemporary non-canonical apocalypses like the Apocalypse of Peter.

Offspring of David, and the bright Morning Star" (22:16; see 2:28). He also promises three times that He is coming soon (22:7, 12, 20). Because Revelation was originally read in the context of worship, the response to Jesus' promise is appropriate. The Hebrew "amen" in Revelation 22:20 is both an affirmation ("so it is") and supplication ("let it be"),[12] affirming the desire that Revelation's message of salvation and judgment be fulfilled. ●

Reflect on this...

What does Jesus' promise to return mean to you?

---

12. Elwell, W. A., & Comfort, P. W. (2001). *Tyndale Bible Dictionary.* Tyndale reference library (35). Wheaton, IL: Tyndale House Publishers.

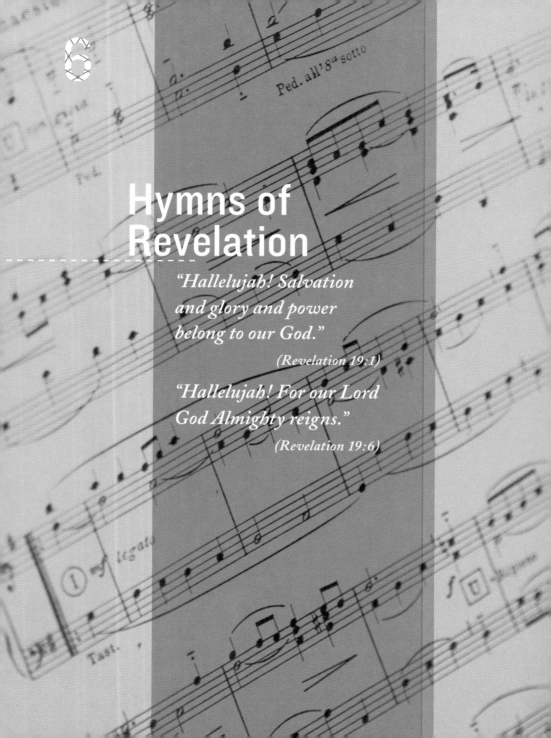

6

Hymns of Revelation

"Hallelujah! Salvation and glory and power belong to our God."

(Revelation 19:1)

"Hallelujah! For our Lord God Almighty reigns."

(Revelation 19:6)

Singing is a universal part of our community worship. Hymns bring special moments of awe and a sense of God's presence in ways that no sermon or teaching can. Ideally, their poetry informs as well as captivates.

Reflect on this...

What are your favorite hymns and/or praise songs? Why are they important to you? How do they make you feel? What theology do they express?

Revelation is full of music, although it was probably more like chanting than the sort of singing we're familiar with. Throughout the book, worshipers say (4:8), sing (5:9), cry out in a loud voice (7:10), and shout (19:1) their praises to God and the Lamb. The singing begins at the center of heaven with the four living creatures (4:8; 5:8; 7:11) and the 24 elders (4:10; 5:8; 7:11; 11:16). They are joined by "thousands upon thousands, and ten thousand times ten thousand" angels (5:11) and finally, every creature in the universe (5:13). The elders sing a new song because the Lamb has redeemed people for God (5:9) and the redeemed themselves sing a new song that only they can sing (14:3).[13]

The hymns they sing give relief in the midst of visions of terror, cries for vengeance, and threats of wrath, but they are not simply emotional outlets. They provide interpretive commentary on John's visions; they both introduce and summarize the narrative. For example, the hymns in chapters 4 and 5 present the majesty of God. This establishes divine authority for judgment in the visions throughout chapters 6-19. The hymns emphasize that praise is due

---

13. The song is new because it celebrates the completely different and miraculous provision by Christ. Only those who are a part of this new life can sing it.

to God and Christ alone rather than to the beast, the Roman imperial cult, or pagan gods. The hymns also highlight the contrast between the universal worship of God and the Lamb and the limited earthly worship of the dragon and the beast (13:4).

The Father and the Lamb are acclaimed for what they have done in behalf of humanity. The Lamb who was slain initiated a new creation and redeems people from all nations and languages. He stands in heaven as the guarantor of victory in God for all who follow Him. In contrast, the beast blasphemes God, makes war against God's people, and seeks to control "every tribe, people, language, and nation" (13:6-7). It is difficult to understand why anyone would choose to worship this enemy, yet people worship both the dragon and the beast and cry out, "Who is like the beast? Who can wage war against it?" (13:4). In the world of the first-century Christians, the economic and political power of the Roman Empire was unrivaled and seemed invincible. That lifestyle was appealing. However, the hymns to God and the Lamb celebrate another reality. They focus on what is true and eternal in a world caught up in the worship of money and power.

Reflect on this...

What does the music we listen to say about our priorities and value system?

What lyrics were most recently running through your mind?

There are many benefits of music, and we may enjoy a variety of styles, but praise music at its best draws us to the very center of heaven. Consider what it would mean if we could join the four living creatures in singing, "Holy, holy, holy is the Lord God Almighty, who was, and is, and is to come" (Revelation 8; see Isaiah 6:3). The use of "holy" three times celebrates God's holiness: God, who is all-powerful, is holy, exceedingly holy. God's power encompasses everything. God created and sustains the universe, and is coming again to dwell forever with those who follow the Lamb. How can we not respond to the heavenly voice who calls us to "Praise our God, all you his servants, you who fear him, both great and small" (19:5)?

> God created and sustains the universe, and is coming again to dwell forever with those who follow the Lamb.

So far we have talked about the hymns as though they were distinctly set apart, perhaps with instructions to the choirmaster like the psalms of the Old Testament, but that is not how they operate in Revelation. The hymns are more like spontaneous outbursts of praise and worship. They have been identified and described in many ways. One such categorization lists them according to type. The *Trisagion* (thrice holy) (4:8) and the invitation to praise (19:5) mentioned above stand alone. The most common type is the victory song (7:10; 11:15; 11:17-18; 12:10-12; 15:3-4; 19:1-2; 19:6-8), followed by those that extoll God's worthiness (4:11; 5:9-10; 5:12), and the doxologies (5:13; 7:12; 16:5-7).[14]

14. Robert H. Smith. "'Worthy is the Lamb' and Other Songs of Revelation." *Currents in Theology and Mission* 25 (1998): 501.

Reflect on this...

Read Revelation 4:8-11. What can we learn about worship from this passage? How does it relate to the way we worship in our churches?

The hymn in chapter 5 is full of theology. Read Revelation 5:9-14 and consider what it teaches about Christ, salvation, and the church. The heavenly choir declares that, like His Father, the Lamb is worthy of praise. Attributing worthiness was a typical feature of Roman hymns to a god, an emperor, or another human patron. The Lamb deserves praise because His sacrifice provides redemption, fellowship, and service to God. Christ's deity is emphasized because He is worthy just as His Father is worthy (see 4:11; 5:12).

The hymn also celebrates the beauty of freedom from sin. It emphasizes the great cost of salvation by including the horror of the slaughter of the Lamb. Theological theories of atonement have tried to explain how Christ's sacrifice provides salvation, but this hymn celebrates its great mystery in metaphorical language. What is not a mystery is who benefits from Christ's sacrifice. People from "every tribe and language and people and nation" are included. Salvation is provided for all without exception. Everyone can enter the kingdom, and all who do so are to serve God. The specifics of that service get to the heart of the Church's role on earth. We are to be priests, mediators between people and God. That's what reigning on earth means. Like the nation of Israel, we are to be a channel of blessing to the world.

In verse 11, the praise escalates as the angels join in worshipping the Lamb. His sacrifice is confirmed as the basis for worship. Their seven-fold acknowledgement of worth includes power and strength that in the Old Testament refer to God's sovereignty (see, for example, Psalm 62:11; Isaiah 45:24). Wealth and wisdom are related to kingship, and honor refers to the respect due a person of worth. Glory and praise are reserved for God alone. This combination, ascribed to the Lamb in verse 12, emphasizes that Jesus is undeniably God.

The hymn concludes in verse 13 with a universal doxology. Metaphorically, every part of creation joins in the crescendo of praise to the Father and the Son. The worship affirms that praise, honor, glory, and power are due God forever. The praise concludes in verse 14 with an affirmation by the four living creatures who began the hymn in verse 9. Their "amen" both confirms the truth of the hymn and invites its continued vocalization. The 24 elders respond by falling down before the throne in worship.

Reflect on this...

Reflect on your response to this hymn. How does it relate to your experiences of corporate worship through singing?

The hymns of Revelation taught the first-century Christians the importance of keeping their focus on the reality of the kingdom of God and the provision for our salvation through the sacrifice of Jesus, the Lamb. This focus counters the tendency to assimilate comfortably into the idolatry of the surrounding culture. The hymns' emphasis on the enduring creative and redeeming power of God and the Lamb strengthened those early Christians who faced persecution and death because of their faith. Those who today experience similar oppression can hold on to that same truth, along with the hope for a better future. Like the Christians in the early Roman Empire, those who live in more prosperous circumstances need to remember that power, wealth, and wisdom belong to the Lamb who was slain. Even when it seems that living a comfortable but compromised life is preferable to following the Lamb in a lifestyle of self-sacrifice, we need to remember that our role in the world is to be priests who bring people to God.

May we join the heavenly choir in singing, "Hallelujah! For our Lord God Almighty reigns" (19:6). The exclamation from the Hebrew literally means, "Praise Yahweh." God who is always sovereign has, through Christ, begun to make that rule known in history. This is not a coercive imposition of power, but an invitation to be who we were created to be, to join in universal praise, to accept our citizenship in God's kingdom here on earth and fulfill our role as priests by bringing people to God. "Hallelujah! Salvation and glory and power belong to our God. . . . Hallelujah! For our Lord God Almighty reigns" (19:1, 6). ●

NOTES:

7

Judgment and Restoration

"I am making everything new!"

(Revelation 21:5)

So far in Revelation we have skirted around its lurid depictions of the punishment of evil, but any reading of the book must recognize that judgment is one of its main themes. It is appropriate that we have waited to deal with this aspect, because it can easily overpower the book's main message of God's beautiful plan for restoration. A reading that focuses on the plagues and the unholy trinity of the dragon and the beasts results in a false view of God. Revelation's fundamental confession of God's unending love and absolute justice brings together the themes of judgment and restoration.

God's governance of the universe ensures that people bear the consequences of their actions. Since the beginning, God has brought order out of chaos. Truth and justice are linked (see 15:3; 16:7; 19:2, 11). God's holiness reveals the truth as it exposes the lies and illusions that disguise evil. The light of truth exposes evil for what it is and what must happen because of it. Judgment is not an external imposition of punishment, but the inevitable consequence of sin.

Reflect on this...

Read Revelation 16:5-6. What guarantees that God's judgments are just?

Revelation's idea of justice follows early Jewish and Christian literature where the principle of *lex talionis* ("measure for measure") is central. The punishment should fit the crime. The idea that those who shed blood must drink blood is a graphic, symbolic statement of the principle that sinful acts have consequences. An often-mistranslated passage also employs the principle of *lex talionis*. A voice from heaven declares that Babylon be given the exact equivalent of her deeds as her punishment (18:6-7a).[15] This is the best kind of punishment because its fairness is obvious even to the wrongdoer.

> **Revelation's fundamental confession of God's unending love and absolute justice brings together the themes of judgment and restoration.**

In John's visions, the judgments come from the throne room in heaven, but in their actual accounts, God does not act directly. The four living creatures summon four riders as the first four seals are opened (6:1, 3, 5, 7) and seven angels blow seven trumpets that announce judgment (8:2, 6). The seven angels who pour out the bowls of God's wrath emerge from the heavenly temple (15:1-6), one of the living creatures gives them the bowls (15:7), and the command to pour the bowls comes from the temple (16:1). The recurring symbol of lightning and thunder accompanies the opening of the seventh seal (8:5), the sounding of the seventh trumpet (11:19), and the pouring out of the seventh bowl (16:18-21). This heavenly display ties judgment with God's holiness since its first mention was in John's vision of the throne room in the center of heaven (4:5a).

The judgments keep coming in three increasingly severe series of seven. This cadence represents the time humanity has to respond to God's calls to repentance. But the people do not respond.

---

15. Here *dipla/diploun* does not mean "twofold" or "twice." It is an expression for "full requital," so a better translation would be "equivalent."

Reflect on this...

Read Revelation 9:20-21. Why do you think people didn't repent? How does it relate to the response of people today?

The plagues and other disasters in John's visions didn't work (see 9:20-21). Fortunately, God has another plan, and this is the central message of Revelation. This letter to the Church[16] calls us to follow the Lamb as faithful witnesses, even to the point of death. This is what will draw the nations to God and to the salvation that is provided through Christ's sacrificial victory. The power to change lives is Christ's sharp two-edged sword that projects from His mouth (1:16; 2:12, 16; 19:15, 21). This symbol of Jesus' faithful witness in His life, teachings, and resurrection judges those who reject God. The final judgment assumes that the suffering witness of Jesus and His Church has brought people to repentance and worship of the true God. The end is deferred so that more may respond to the Church's witness.

The end is delayed, but there *will* be an end to evil. John identifies this evil in the metaphor of a dragon that is the "ancient serpent called the devil, or Satan" (12:9; also see 20:2). These designations require further unpacking. The Greek word for "devil" means "slanderer," and the Greek for "Satan" means "adversary" or "accuser." This chief opponent in John's visions obstructs God's design and makes war with angels and humans, slandering the saints and deceiving the world. The dragon is joined by a beast from the sea, whose

---

16. Remember that Revelation is a letter addressed to seven churches that represent the universal church (see chapter 1 of our study).

number is 666 (13:1-3, 18), and has been popularized as the "Antichrist."[17] Another beast comes up from the land and is known as "the false prophet" (13:11-15; 16:13; 19:20; 20:10). These three form an unholy trinity that tries to seize God's power and influence over humanity. The nature of this false god contrasts dramatically with the powerful, holy, loving, and merciful triune God who created and sustains the universe and plans a new heaven and earth where people bask in divine light and love. In contrast, the unholy trio represents oppressive and unjust forces that have been partially fulfilled by historical figures and institutions throughout the centuries. Their end is the lake of fire along with Death and Hades, the personification of death.

Reflect on this...

Read Revelation 19:20 and 20:14. What does this end of evil and death mean to you?

The death of death and evil makes way for the restoration of God's perfect plan for humanity. John describes "'a new heaven and a new earth'" with the New Jerusalem coming down to earth as a Bride (21:1-2). This beautiful woman-city metaphor contrasts sharply with the destroyed harlot Babylon. It is both a place and a relationship with no more death, mourning, crying, or pain. The water of life flows freely in the presence of God.

---

17. Remember, though, that the term "Antichrist" does not appear in Revelation. See 1 John 2:18,22; 4:3; and 2 John 1:7.

Reflect on this...

Read Revelation 21:1-7. How does this vision make you feel? How would you describe a reality in which there is no evil or death and where God's presence is a constant reality?

This wonderful promise is verified by God's declaration, "I am making everything new!" (21:5). The Greek verb form emphasizes the certainty of this future that is grounded in the Creator's ongoing provision as well as the sacrificial victory of the Lamb. The identification of the speaker as the Alpha and Omega (21:6; see also 1:8) guarantees God's truthfulness, trustworthiness, faithfulness, and power to complete what He has set in motion. God's speech continues with a statement like that of Jesus on the cross (John 19:30): "It is done" (Revelation 21:6). There is no other sacrifice, no other provision that must be put in place. We are not desperately fighting a war against evil. We know the outcome because we know the One who guarantees it. We wait for that time as faithful witnesses, priests who draw people to life in the presence of God.

The responsibility to live as priests who represent Christ to the world can be heavy at times. People do not always respond. Less demanding lifestyles hold false promises of enjoyment and ease. There may be persecution. But if we keep our focus on God, we "will inherit all this" (21:7).

After these assurances and a warning to unbelievers, John is taken to a high mountain where he sees the fulfillment of God's promises. Language fails him as he struggles to express the magnificent, otherworldly beauty of the

New Jerusalem, and he continues to use symbolism to do so. For example, the cube of 12,000 stadia (about 1,400 miles) represents the city's perfection.[18] The area is roughly that of the first-century Roman Empire and suggests a worldwide response to the gospel. Its height draws heaven and earth together in spatial imagery, and this incredibly large cube that represents God's presence gives free access to God, in contrast to the limited access to the small four-square Holy of Holies in the earthly temple. God's presence makes the city radiant, and since the city represents the saints, they reflect the glory of life in God's presence. The river and trees in the center of the New Jerusalem represent the Garden of Eden. It is paradise regained, but better because the tree of life is not restricted. Its leaves are "for the healing of the nations" (22:2). The constantly open gates on each side of the city symbolize universal access; everyone who turns from evil may enter God's presence.

Reflect on this...

Read Revelation 21:9—22:5. What speaks to you from this vision?

After this magnificent vision, there is a final warning of the consequences of sin and a four-fold invitation to come: two are addressed to Christ, to come and fulfill His glorious promise, and two are addressed to the world to repent and receive these blessings. The final "amen" is both an affirmation of the book's message and a supplication that God's judgment and restoration be fulfilled. Amen. ●

---

18. See the discussion of numbers in the chapter on symbolism.

NOTES:

NOTES:

Other Dialog studies also available!

FAITH AMONG FRIENDS
Creating Intentional Conversations

How should people of faith live among the unfaithful? How will non-Christians see the love of God in our lives? *Faith Among Friends* reveals the many ways our lives as Christians testify to who the Lord is, what he has to say, and how he can change lives.

PARTICIPANT'S GUIDE ISBN: 978-0-8341-3139-2
FACILITATOR'S GUIDE ISBN: 978-0-8341-3140-8

SUIT UP
Putting on the Full Armor of God

The armor of God is a fantastic metaphor for how we are to live our lives as Christians. We are fighting a war against the unseen enemy of our souls. *Suit Up* will guide you through God's armor as described in Ephesians 6:10-18 and help you discover how each piece is designed to protect and strengthen your spiritual life.

PARTICIPANT'S GUIDE ISBN: 978-0-8341-3141-5
FACILITATOR'S GUIDE ISBN: 978-0-8341-3142-2

Available online at DialogSeries.com